THE
BLESSED
LIFE

four principles God promises to honor

KEN McCOY

Copyright © 2012 by Striving Together Publications.
All Scripture quotations are taken from
the King James Version.

First published in 2012 by Striving Together Publications, a ministry
of Lancaster Baptist Church, Lancaster, CA 93535. Striving Together
Publications is committed to providing tried, trusted, and proven
resources that will further equip local churches to carry out the
Great Commission. Your comments and suggestions are valued.

All rights reserved. No part of this book may be reproduced, stored
in a retrieval system, or transmitted in any form or by any means—
electronic, mechanical, photocopy, recording, or otherwise—
without written permission of the publisher, except for brief
quotations in printed reviews.

Striving Together Publications
4020 E. Lancaster Blvd.
Lancaster, CA 93535
800.201.7748
www.strivingtogether.com

Cover design by Andrew Hutchens
Layout by Craig Parker
Edited by Monica Bass
Special thanks to our proofreaders

The author and publication team have put forth every effort to give proper
credit to quotes and thoughts that are not original with the author. It is not
our intent to claim originality with any quote or thought that could not
readily be tied to an original source.

ISBN 978-1-59894-198-2
Printed in the United States of America

Contents

Introduction v

Principle One
A Good Man Obtains Favor 1

Principle Two
A Faithful Man Abounds with Blessing 17

Principle Three
A Trusting Man Gets Direction 39

Principle Four
A Giving Man Prospers 49

Conclusion 61

Introduction

I was raised in the coal fields of West Virginia, and as you might imagine, we were poor—like nearly everyone else in the coal camp. My four brothers and I never *felt* poor, however, because we had loving, Christian parents, and we had each other.

My granddad worked in the mines, my dad worked in the mines, and it only seemed logical that I would follow in their footsteps. So I became a third generation coal miner.

When I was seventeen years old, however, my life changed. Although I had been raised in a Christian home, I had never personally trusted Christ as my Saviour. But on Sunday, November 29, 1970, I asked Christ to save me.

From the moment I was saved, God changed my life in a powerful way. Not only did He give me a home in Heaven, but He planted in my heart a burning desire to serve Him.

Shortly after I was saved, I was given an opportunity to teach a Sunday school class. At the age of eighteen with very little Bible knowledge and even less experience, I was completely unqualified for this position. But I was thrilled for the privilege, and I poured my heart into it.

I began to study God's Word with intensity. I would read a passage, and when I came to a verse I couldn't understand, I'd stop and look it up in the commentary that my dad gave me. I never had formal Bible training, but I did learn to dig into Scripture for myself. If I wanted to be effective in those kids' lives each Sunday, I had no choice but to study diligently and persistently.

Introduction

I've been studying and teaching God's Word for over forty years now. To be honest, there are parts of the Bible that I still don't understand; and there are some parts that I probably will not understand until I meet Christ face to face.

Yet, as I have studied God's Word through the years, I have determined not to focus on what I don't understand, but rather to hone in on God's clear promises and claim them for myself.

All throughout Scripture, God offers, "If you will _____, I will _____." These are called "conditional promises." They are God's proposal to bless us if we will fulfill the condition that He specifies.

When an omnipotent (all-powerful), omniscient (all-knowing), sovereign God wants to enter into a covenant with me, I think it is foolish to ignore it. So, as a teenage boy, I simply decided to believe God and take Him up on His offers. With a child-like faith, I decided to claim the promises He made and live by the principles He set forth for them.

Over forty years later, I'm thankful I did. When God offers a conditional promise, He never specifies an impossible condition; and He always keeps His Word. What an opportunity for us as His people to prove His faithfulness and experience His blessing!

There are four principles in particular that I found early in my Christian walk that I decided to base my life and service around. These are simple, easy-to-understand truths that any Christian can choose to live by.

These four principles are the subject of this book. You can claim them by faith and live them with confidence.

God's Word is true. These principles would be true even if I said they weren't, yet I can add my testimony of experience to validate them. As I have learned to live these four principles, I have seen God keep His Word—over and over again.

So, as we look at these four guiding principles, I challenge you to claim the promises of each of them for your own!

1
Principle One

A Good Man Obtains Favor

One of the first books of the Bible that I fell in love with as a teenager was Proverbs. I loved how plainly God laid out His principles for life through these chapters.

When I came across Proverbs 12:2, I was amazed at the promise of this verse: "A good man obtaineth favour of the Lord: but a man of wicked devices will he condemn."

I kept pondering the phrase, "A good man obtaineth favour."

I have every reason to be thankful that God is no respecter of persons (Acts 10:34). He loves poor coal miners just the same as wealthy politicians. If as a seventeen-year-old I had been required to climb up a religious or social ladder for God to save me, I would still be lost. I praise God that the gift of salvation is for all who are willing to receive Christ. Jesus gave His life for all of mankind, and He loves each one of us equally.

And yet, some men especially obtain God's favor. How?

Real People, Real Favor

Throughout Scripture, God specifically points out several people with special terms of recognition:

- God called Abraham "the Friend of God" (James 2:23).
- God called Job "perfect and upright" (Job 1:1).
- God called David "a man after mine own heart" (Acts 13:22).
- God called Daniel "greatly beloved" (Daniel 10:11).

Were these men God's favorites? No, but they did have God's favor on their lives.

Like you and me, these men were sinners. Romans 3:12 plainly tells us, "They are all gone out of the way, they are together become unprofitable; there is none that doeth good, no, not one."

These men were ordinary people who had a heart for God. They weren't perfect men, but they were good men—men who loved God and decided to live for Him.

This is encouraging! When we look at the lives of these men, we see that God blesses ordinary people who have made a simple decision to live for Him.

Make a Choice

The men mentioned above who had the favor of God on their lives all had a common denominator—they said "no" to the world and its pull on their lives.

At the call of God, Abraham left everything he knew—his family, hometown, security—to travel to a country he didn't know. God promised Abraham that

He would bless him, and Abraham took God at His word. Hebrews 11:8 records, "By faith Abraham, when he was called to go out into a place which he should after receive for an inheritance, obeyed; and he went out, not knowing whither he went."

Job was a godly man who also happened to be the most prosperous man in the East. But when God allowed Satan to take Job's wealth, family, and even his health, Job persisted in trusting God. His wife despairingly said, "Curse God and die" (Job 2:9). But Job replied, "What? shall we receive good at the hand of God, and shall we not receive evil?" (Job 2:10). Job restated this commitment later with the words, "Though he slay me, yet will I trust in him" (Job 13:15).

David, a teenage shepherd boy, rejected the pull of an entire army of fearful soldiers, bravely taking a stand for God. You will remember from 1 Samuel 17 that David's father sent him out to bring supplies to his brothers who were on the front lines of an ongoing battle. When David arrived, he watched as the giant Goliath blasphemed God and ridiculed the Israelites' cowardice to fight him. Unable to let God's name be shamed, David stepped forward and killed the giant with a stone hurled from a shepherd's slingshot.

When Daniel was ripped from his family and homeland, and carried captive to Babylon, he still chose to honor God. Faced with the command to eat meat against the Old Testament laws, "Daniel purposed in his heart that he would not defile himself with the portion of the king's meat, nor with the wine which he drank" (Daniel 1:8).

In every case, God blessed the choice of these men with His favor. For you and me, the points at which we must boldly stand for Christ come in different settings. But it is always a clear choice.

Often, the choice is difficult. I learned this as a young Christian.

Although I was a third-generation coal miner, I decided early on that I wanted to work my way up in the industry. Shortly after I was saved, I was sent to a meeting for my job in Charleston, West Virginia.

Our session broke for lunch, and the guys I was with suggested we go out together for a meal. Of course, most coal miners aren't exactly a Sunday school-attending bunch. These guys cuss, swear, fight, and drink with experience.

We walked down the street, and the guys stopped in front of a bar. This wasn't a restaurant that happened to sell beer; it was a bar.

At that moment, God's Spirit spoke directly to me with one word, "No." I knew I couldn't go in.

"Sorry, fellas, I can't go in there."

"Oh, come on," they protested. "We're not even going to drink. We're just getting lunch."

There I stood surrounded by a group of important people—some of whom would play a vital role in my advancement in the coal industry—and I had to decide if I would say "yes" to them or say "yes" to the Holy Spirit. Frankly, I wanted to rationalize away God's prompting. Yet, His voice had been clear.

"You guys go ahead; I'm not going in."

They went in, and I found a restaurant down the street for my meal. Forty years later, I'm thankful for that choice. It kept me in the place of God's favor. Even though it seemed difficult at the moment, it was worth it. God's favor is far more valuable than a moment of acceptance.

Even when we successfully say "no" to the world once, Satan continues to tempt us with sin. His goal is to ruin our testimony and cause us to choose to forfeit God's favor.

Just a few years ago, I was faced with a temptation similar to the one I had faced in Charleston. This time, however, it was in Ukraine.

God had blessed me, and I worked my way up through the ranks of the coal mines. By 2005, I went out on my own with some other guys, and we started our own coal company. The company grew quickly, and just three years later, we sold it for enough profit that I was able to retire.

As part of the sale proceedings, we flew to Ukraine to sign papers with the buyers of our company. Like many Eastern European nations, drinking vodka is common in Ukraine. One of my partners in business foresaw that I wouldn't want to drink, so before we left, he tried to explain the situation.

"Ken, over in Ukraine, they toast for everything. They toast for a wedding, and they toast for something as simple as a nice day outside. Especially, they toast for purchasing a coal company."

I was the vice-president of operations, and I knew that my partner didn't want me to cause any embarrassment to myself, my co-workers, or the Ukrainians. After he finished explaining the situation to me, I said to him, "I am sorry, but you know I don't drink. I've never taken a drink in my life, and I'm not going to go against my convictions now." My business partners are good men, and they have always respected my relationship with the Lord.

"Ken, you still don't understand. The Ukrainians will be offended if you don't drink."

"I'm sorry, I don't want to offend them. But if this is my only alternative, I guess they will have to be offended. I'm not drinking."

My partner was right. The Ukrainians did drink a lot—every time we went out with them. When I turned down the drink, they would look at each other and shake their heads. "Religious," they would mutter.

But I knew this was a simple choice to obey God and claim His favor.

What It Takes

Remember, the promise to obtain God's favor comes with a condition. "A good man obtaineth favour." Every Christian would like to have God's favor, but we aren't always willing to make the choices to be "a good man."

One of the clearest examples in Scripture of men who valued God's favor more than their own lives were the three Hebrew children—Hananiah, Mishael, and Azariah. We usually remember them by their Babylonian names—Shadrach, Meshach, and Abednego.

The king erected an idol that stood ninety feet tall, and he held a ceremony in its honor. Attendance to the ceremony was required, and the king commanded everyone present to bow before his statue.

But while the crowd bowed, three lone figures remained standing. These godly men loyally obeyed

God's command "Thou shalt have no other gods before me" (Exodus 20:3). Their silent but public declaration of loyalty to God incited the violent anger of the king. He had already promised a painful death in the fiery furnace to anyone who dared defy his command. The king called the men before him and gave them one more chance to bow, followed by a vehement threat:

> *Then Nebuchadnezzar in his rage and fury commanded to bring Shadrach, Meshach, and Abednego. Then they brought these men before the king. Nebuchadnezzar spake and said unto them, Is it true, O Shadrach, Meshach, and Abednego, do not ye serve my gods, nor worship the golden image which I have set up? Now if ye be ready that at what time ye hear the sound of the cornet, flute, harp, sackbut, psaltery, and dulcimer, and all kinds of musick, ye fall down and worship the image which I have made; well: but if ye worship not, ye shall be cast the same hour into the midst of a burning fiery furnace; and who is*

that God that shall deliver you out of my hands?
—Daniel 3:13–15

In contrast to the king's fury, Shadrach, Meshach, and Abednego answered in a calm and deliberate tone, the result of hearts already settled on God:

Shadrach, Meshach, and Abednego, answered and said to the king, O Nebuchadnezzar, we are not careful to answer thee in this matter. If it be so, our God whom we serve is able to deliver us from the burning fiery furnace, and he will deliver us out of thine hand, O king. But if not, be it known unto thee, O king, that we will not serve thy gods, nor worship the golden image which thou hast set up.
—Daniel 3:16–18

I love the steadfast and determined focus of these men. When it came to a choice about whether or not they would stand for God, they were firm—"If we live or die, we are going to remain faithful to God."

In this case, God blessed the men's choice with life, preserving them in the fire and delivering them from the furnace. But regardless of the outcome, their choice was made: "We won't bow."

This is the choice of a good man.

If you choose to stand for God, people will ridicule, slight, criticize, malign, and persecute you. But God will bless you with His favor, and this is worth more than the favor of all other men combined.

As I often remind my two sons, it's okay to be different. People may ridicule you at your moment of choice, but ultimately, they will respect and admire you. As God blesses you with His favor, others will recognize His hand on your life, and even those who once poked fun at you will come to you when they need the Lord.

A Basis for Optimism

The promise of God's favor is not a guarantee for a pain-free life, and it's not a "health and prosperity" message. But it is an absolute promise of blessing.

My coworkers used to tell me, "Ken, you're the most optimistic person we've ever seen." They may have been right. I have every reason for hope and encouragement because I claim God's favor. Basically, I figure that if an omnipotent God is on my side, I'm going to win. If I set out to do something, I'm going to be successful. If I embark on an endeavor, I expect it to flourish. I know that I'm unqualified and incapable for much of what God has allowed me to do, but I serve a capable God.

As a teenager, I decided to take God up on His Proverbs 12:2 bargain. He promised, "A good man obtaineth favor." And I purposed to be "a good man." It's as simple as that.

Like Abraham, Job, David, and Daniel, you too, can experience God's favor in your life. Choose to walk with God and to stand for God, and you can expect God to bless you. Being "a good man" often requires a willingness to resist the world's temptation, but God always blesses this choice with His special favor.

2
Principle Two

A Faithful Man Abounds
with Blessing

Shortly after I was saved, a flood swept through the hills of West Virginia and carried everything we owned with it. I was left with only the clothes that I was wearing—a t-shirt, a pair of jeans, and old tennis shoes. I didn't have a dime in the bank, and the next set of clothes I received was from the Salvation Army. I was so excited to get that second pair of jeans—until I found out that the zipper didn't work!

When I look at my background, I know without a doubt that any blessing in my life has come from

God's hand. I am a poor country boy from the coal mines of West Virginia, and God has blessed my life beyond my wildest dreams.

I learned as a young Christian that although God's blessing is undeserved, it is not unpromised. In Proverbs 28:20, God gives us another promise to claim: "A faithful man shall abound with blessings: but he that maketh haste to be rich shall not be innocent."

Think of it! An omnipotent God who holds the universe in His hand and owns everything that you see has the ability to bless you abundantly. He simply promises, "If you will be faithful, I will not only give you a blessing, but I will make you to abound with blessings."

An Easy Condition

I'm thankful that in this conditional promise God offers to bless faithfulness rather than talent. If God's blessings on our lives were dependent on our intelligence, talent, or ability, we would all be

Principle 2—A Faithful Man Abounds with Blessing

limited. (Some of us would hit those limits sooner than others!)

But faithfulness is a trait that anyone can possess. It doesn't require unique education or ability. It just requires character.

Over and over, in both the Old and the New Testaments, Scripture commends the quality of faithfulness in God's servants:

- **Moses:** "My servant Moses is not so, who is faithful in all mine house" (Numbers 12:7).
- **Samuel:** "And I will raise me up a faithful priest, that shall do according to that which is in mine heart and in my mind: and I will build him a sure house; and he shall walk before mine anointed for ever" (1 Samuel 2:35).
- **David:** "Then Ahimelech answered the king, and said, And who is so faithful among all thy servants as David, which is the king's son in law, and goeth at thy bidding, and is honourable in thine house?" (1 Samuel 22:14).

- **Temple Workmen:** "Howbeit there was no reckoning made with them of the money that was delivered into their hand, because they dealt faithfully" (2 Kings 22:7).
- **Hanani:** "That I gave my brother Hanani, and Hananiah the ruler of the palace, charge over Jerusalem: for he was a faithful man, and feared God above many" (Nehemiah 7:2).
- **Treasurers:** "And I made treasurers over the treasuries, Shelemiah the priest, and Zadok the scribe, and of the Levites, Pedaiah: and next to them was Hanan the son of Zaccur, the son of Mattaniah: for they were counted faithful, and their office was to distribute unto their brethren" (Nehemiah 13:13).
- **Uriah and Zechariah:** "And I took unto me faithful witnesses to record, Uriah the priest, and Zechariah the son of Jeberechiah" (Isaiah 8:2).
- **Daniel:** "Then the presidents and princes sought to find occasion against Daniel concerning the kingdom; but they could find

none occasion nor fault; forasmuch as he was faithful, neither was there any error or fault found in him" (Daniel 6:4).
- **Epaphras:** "As ye also learned of Epaphras our dear fellowservant, who is for you a faithful minister of Christ" (Colossians 1:7).
- **Tychicus:** "All my state shall Tychicus declare unto you, who is a beloved brother, and a faithful minister and fellowservant in the Lord" (Colossians 4:7).
- **Onesimus:** "With Onesimus, a faithful and beloved brother, who is one of you. They shall make known unto you all things which are done here" (Colossians 4:9).
- **Silvanus:** "By Silvanus, a faithful brother unto you, as I suppose, I have written briefly, exhorting, and testifying that this is the true grace of God wherein ye stand" (1 Peter 5:12).
- **Gaius:** "Beloved, thou doest faithfully whatsoever thou doest to the brethren, and to strangers" (3 John 1:5).

Some of the people listed in the verses above are not well-known or oft-remembered by us. Yet, their defining trait and that which brought them blessing was the trait of faithfulness.

The Road Less Traveled

This promise that God will bless faithfulness is so basic that anyone can understand it. It's not theologically complicated or deep. Yet, few decide to claim it.

To be faithful to God usually requires that you forfeit the acceptance of the crowd. Faithfully walking with God often means that you forgo being "one of the gang."

Christ calls us to a narrow road.

Enter ye in at the strait gate: for wide is the gate, and broad is the way, that leadeth to destruction, and many there be which go in thereat: Because strait is the gate, and narrow is the way, which leadeth unto life, and few there be that find it.
—Matthew 7:13–14

Notice that you must enter this narrow road through the straight gate. This gate refers to salvation through Christ alone. In John 14:6, Jesus stated, "I am the way, the truth, and the life: no man cometh unto the Father, but by me." Faithfulness to a religion means nothing; trusting in Christ is everything.

Once a person has trusted Christ for salvation, there is a temptation to base Christian growth on another person or a godly figure you look up to. People, however, are fallible, and they often disappoint. The only way to walk in faithfulness throughout your entire journey is to walk trusting in Christ alone. Walk in confidence of His promises, trusting His faithfulness.

Faithful to the End

Over the forty-two years that I've been walking with the Lord, I have seen many come and go. I've seen people start out to be pastors, youth leaders, soulwinners, Sunday school teachers, and serve in a variety of other capacities. Sadly, I've also seen many quit.

Many years ago, I purposed in my heart that I was going to be faithful until the end. Like every other Christian, I have experienced setbacks and roadblocks along the way, but God has also blessed me with abundant blessings.

Satan will do all that he can to discourage the Christian who has determined to live faithfully, and he will work to get us to focus on the difficulties rather than on the blessings.

I remember once when I was going door-to-door in my community inviting people to our church's revival service. I was probably in my early twenties at the time.

I was surprised when one door opened, and one of my former schoolteachers stood on the other side. I invited him to the meeting—just like I had his neighbors. I sort of expected that he would say, "No, thank you, I'm not interested." But he didn't. He just laughed and closed the door.

Rejection I could have handled, but ridicule was tough. In that moment, I had to remember that I was serving Christ who is more important than my former teacher will ever be. Christ's approval matters most.

Since that day, I've experienced many other discouraging or disheartening circumstances while serving the Lord. Yet, I often remember the patriarchs of old that stood tests of severe persecution—greater tests than I have even come close to facing—faithfully.

If you want God's blessing for faithfulness, remember that you must commit now to be faithful to the end. Remember, too, that the blessings far outweigh the burdens. God promises that He will make the faithful man to abound with blessings!

As the Apostle Paul neared the end of his life, he could look back and know he had been faithful: "I have fought a good fight, I have finished my course, I have kept the faith" (2 Timothy 4:7).

Matthew 25:21 reminds us that faithfulness is a quality that Christ is looking for. Like the servant in this verse, I want to hear my Lord say, "Well done, thou good and faithful servant."

The Greatest Tests of Faithfulness

The most significant tests of our faithfulness are adversity and prosperity.

The greatest test of faithfulness up to this point in my life was undoubtedly the time of my greatest loss. My wife, Peggy, and I were faithful and active in our church. She sang in the choir, we both taught classes, and we were involved in just about every available opportunity for ministry.

When the Lord blessed us with a set of twin boys, we were thrilled, and we purposed above all to raise our children to serve the Lord. My wife was blessed to be a stay-at-home mother, and she used her time to invest totally in our children. This was vitally important to both of us. Proverbs 22:6 says, "Train up a child in the way he should go: and when he is old, he will not depart from it." We believed this with all our hearts. By the time Jason and Jeremy were talking, they were quoting Bible verses and could answer questions about many Bible stories we had read to them.

Soon after the twins' second birthday, we learned that Peggy was once again expecting—another baby boy. Before his birth, we named him Matthew, which means "a gift from God." Little did we know how precious this gift would be to us.

Shortly before Matthew's due date, we entered a storm of adversity that I don't even like to think about, let alone write about. To this day, I can hardly stand to recall it.

That Thursday had been a stormy, dreary day outside. Inside, there was no electricity, but Peggy had created a fun day for Jason and Jeremy. All morning they played, and then they sat together in an oversized rocking chair that held all three of them. (Actually, the chair held all four of them. Peggy was scheduled to deliver Matthew by C-section the following Monday.) Peggy often held the boys in that chair and reviewed Bible stories and memory verses with them.

As they reviewed that day, the boys answered all of Peggy's questions and actually wanted to tell the stories to her. Jeremy, the oldest twin, recited Psalm 23 and asked his mother to sing a song he loved titled

"I'm Going Home Where I Belong." Although it was a dreary and gloomy day, what a blessing that time spent with our sons would turn out to be for my wife.

When I walked in the door that evening, Jason and Jeremy were as excited as always to see their dad. They knew that while Mommy cooked, we had playtime! But as the twins bounded down the stairs to the playroom, Jeremy had a serious fall.

We rushed Jeremy to the nearest hospital, but he was becoming comatose and had to be transferred by ambulance to a trauma hospital. We arrived at the trauma hospital where he was immediately taken into surgery and then put on life support.

While Jeremy was in surgery at the further hospital, Peggy went into early labor and gave birth to our youngest son at our local hospital. I didn't get to see Matthew—our special gift from God—until eight days later.

In the meantime, we prayed fervently for Jeremy's healing. Ten days after the accident, which was one day after Jeremy's third birthday, he was taken off life support. As I held him in my arms, he went to be with the Lord.

I cannot describe the anguish of losing a child. It seemed to Peggy and me that our hearts were literally breaking, being torn right out of our bodies. In the midst of the pain, Satan tempted me to quit. He tempted me to respond in angry defiance toward God—to somehow "get back" at Him by quitting on Him.

When you are grieving, you don't think rationally—you just hurt. No person, no words, nothing can help you in any way to find peace—except for God and His sweet Holy Spirit.

In this vulnerable time, when I honestly wanted to quit, the Lord reminded me of His promise to bless faithfulness. Peggy knew deep in her heart that this wasn't the time to quit. Where could one go? Nothing could help us except the sweet comfort of the Holy Spirit. He filled Peggy's heart, helping her to accept as well as she could what God had taken from us. And by God's grace, I also committed to remain faithful to our Lord through this trial.

Years later, I'm so thankful we didn't quit. Not only is our Heavenly Father worthy of our faithfulness, but looking back, I can see how He sustained us every step of the way through this dark valley. He brought the comfort and healing to our hearts that no human can give.

If you are in your own season of adversity, let me challenge you—be faithful. Adversity always makes us more vulnerable to the temptation to quit on God. Resist Satan's suggestions to blame God, and choose instead to hope in Him and cling to His promises. Not only will you be glad you did when you look back years later, but even now—in the midst of your most painful moments—you can experience the grace of God when you faithfully trust Him.

Adversity, however, isn't the only test of faithfulness. Prosperity can be just as fatal. In adversity, we want to quit; in prosperity, we tend to forget.

When life is going well—everyone is healthy, the bills are paid, there is money in the bank, and the future looks rosy—we think that we don't need to depend on God. Strange as it may seem, it is on our best days that the devil most successfully lures us into depending on our own strength and the power of our own resources.

One of the most tragic examples in the Bible of a man who failed the test of prosperity is King Uzziah. Uzziah inherited a collapsing kingdom, made shaky by unfaithful kings. Scripture records Uzziah wholeheartedly following after God. In fact, as he sought the Lord, "God made him to prosper" (2 Chronicles 26:5). The kingdom of Judah once again flourished under his godly leadership. Scripture records, "And his name spread far abroad; for he was marvelouslly helped, till he was strong" (2 Chronicles 26:15).

But it was that very flourishing—that point of prosperity—that was Uzziah's ruin. For "when he was strong, his heart was lifted up to his destruction" (2 Chronicles 26:16). Uzziah forgot that his prosperity was not of his own making—it was God's blessing. He quit relying on the Lord and was no longer faithful. The tragic result was that, "Uzziah the king was a leper unto the day of his death" (2 Chronicles 26:21).

When we pause to think about it, we *always* need God. On our worst days, we need God's help and strength. On our best days, we need His continued blessing. And yet, it is during these two extremes that we are most likely to forsake Him.

When you face either of these two tests of faithfulness, remember to be faithful to your God. And especially, remember His faithfulness to you.

Great Is His Faithfulness

We noted earlier several Bible characters who were faithful. Yet, for every verse in Scripture that speaks of the faithfulness of a man, there are many more which speak of the faithfulness of our God. Consider just a few:

> *Know therefore that the LORD thy God, he is God, the faithful God, which keepeth covenant and mercy with them that love him and keep his commandments to a thousand generations;*
> —DEUTERONOMY 7:9

Principle 2—A Faithful Man Abounds with Blessing

Thy mercy, O L<small>ORD</small>, is in the heavens; and thy faithfulness reacheth unto the clouds.—P<small>SALM</small> 36:5

O L<small>ORD</small> God of hosts, who is a strong L<small>ORD</small> like unto thee? or to thy faithfulness round about thee?—P<small>SALM</small> 89:8

Thy faithfulness is unto all generations: thou hast established the earth, and it abideth. —P<small>SALM</small> 119:90

It is of the L<small>ORD</small>'s mercies that we are not consumed, because his compassions fail not. They are new every morning: great is thy faithfulness. —L<small>AMENTATIONS</small> 3:22–23

God is faithful, by whom ye were called unto the fellowship of his Son Jesus Christ our Lord. —1 C<small>ORINTHIANS</small> 1:9

Faithful is he that calleth you, who also will do it.—1 T<small>HESSALONIANS</small> 5:24

But the Lord is faithful, who shall stablish you, and keep you from evil.—2 T<small>HESSALONIANS</small> 3:3

If we believe not, yet he abideth faithful: he cannot deny himself.—2 TIMOTHY 2:13

Wherefore in all things it behoved him to be made like unto his brethren, that he might be a merciful and faithful high priest in things pertaining to God, to make reconciliation for the sins of the people.
—HEBREWS 2:17

Wherefore let them that suffer according to the will of God commit the keeping of their souls to him in well doing, as unto a faithful Creator.
—1 PETER 4:19

If we confess our sins, he is faithful and just to forgive us our sins, and to cleanse us from all unrighteousness.—1 JOHN 1:9

And from Jesus Christ, who is the faithful witness, and the first begotten of the dead, and the prince of the kings of the earth. Unto him that loved us, and washed us from our sins in his own blood,
—REVELATION 1:5

> *And I saw heaven opened, and behold a white horse; and he that sat upon him was called Faithful and True, and in righteousness he doth judge and make war.*—REVELATION 19:11

From just this sampling of verses that speak of God's faithfulness, we see that for every need of our lives and in every season of our service, God is faithful to us. Thus, our faithfulness to Him is sustained by His faithfulness to us!

Just Do It

God's promise is simple: "You be faithful, and I will bless you abundantly." First Corinthians 4:2 reminds us, "Moreover it is required in stewards, that a man be found faithful." You and I are stewards of the life that God has given us. We must faithfully return that life to Him one day at a time.

Aren't you thankful that God doesn't promise to bless the most talented or capable? He simply instructs us to be faithful. This is a simple choice—we just do it.

God seeks servants who have a willing heart and a committed spirit. Purpose in your heart to be faithful, and watch God's blessings in your life abound.

3
Principle Three

A Trusting Man Gets Direction

Perhaps one of the most familiar passages in Scripture is Proverbs 3:5–6: "Trust in the Lord with all thine heart; and lean not unto thine own understanding. In all thy ways acknowledge him, and he shall direct thy paths."

We often use these verses as a reminder to fully trust God. But I think sometimes we are slow to claim the promise these verses deliver of God's absolute direction. Like the other two principles that we have already examined, these verses are conditional promises from God: if we will trust Him, He promises to provide direction.

Sure Steps

In Proverbs 3:5–6, the God who holds the world together promises that if we trust His direction, He will guide us aright. In Psalm 37:23–24, God further assures, "The steps of a good man are ordered by the Lord: and he delighteth in his way. Though he fall, he shall not be utterly cast down: for the Lord upholdeth him with his hand."

This promise gives us confidence—not in ourselves, but in God. We can walk with sure steps, trusting that He is guiding us.

Nearly every day of my life, for the past forty years, I have prayed, "Lord, please give me Your direction. Tell me what You want me to do." And then I follow where He leads.

Notice the certainty of God's promise: "he shall direct thy paths." He doesn't say "I might direct you" or "I probably will." He doesn't mislead us or play

Principle 3—A Trusting Man Gets Direction

games with us. He truly desires to guide and direct our paths. When we are walking with Him and seeking His direction, He will lead us.

Years ago, when I found this incredible promise of God's direction, I decided to believe it and confidently walk in its security. The Lord knows that I am sincerely willing to follow wherever He leads, so I have determined to unhesitatingly go full speed ahead through open doors.

Of course, there are some decision points that are difficult. Sometimes it is tough to know the Lord's will, but even then, I don't linger in indecision for very long. Many times I've prayed, "Lord, close doors You want closed, and open doors that You want open. I'm following You through open doors."

Confidence in God's promise to direct our steps gives us boldness and surety as we move forward for God. When I walk through a door which I believe God has opened, I don't look back, because I trust that He has guided my steps.

Who Knows?

Part of the reason that we struggle with claiming this promise is because when we walk through an open door and then run into adversity, we assume the problems came because we weren't following God's direction. But this is not necessarily the case.

In Isaiah 30:21, God promises to give us direction as we walk: "And thine ears shall hear a word behind thee, saying, This is the way, walk ye in it, when ye turn to the right hand, and when ye turn to the left."

But too often the scenario goes like this: We ask God for guidance. We hear His voice directing us in a particular direction. We move in that direction. Adversity comes, and we wonder if we should have gone the other way.

Second guessing God's leading because of problems is foolish. The truth is, worse problems may have come had we turned the other way! We don't know the outcome of every choice; that is why we follow God's leading in the first place.

Principle 3—A Trusting Man Gets Direction

Trusting the Lord to direct our paths means that we do not rely on circumstantial evidence to put His leading on trial. It means we simply trust Him and leave the outcomes to His sovereignty.

Think of the life of Joseph. He trusted God, and yet it seemed that at every turn, Joseph's problems became worse! Genesis 39–50 records Joseph's incredible and intricate story.

Joseph trusted the dreams God gave him and shared them with his brothers. This landed Joseph first in a pit and then in slave shackles.

Joseph trusted God and followed His commands by resisting the temptation to moral impurity. This path led Joseph to prison.

Joseph faithfully served even in the prison, still trusting God to bring him out eventually. Yet, when Joseph's hope grew brightest, he was forgotten by the one he had helped, and by all outer appearances, it seemed Joseph would spend the rest of his life in prison.

And yet, in one day, Joseph's entire situation changed. He moved from the prison to the palace.

By the end of the day, he was second in command of the entire nation of Egypt. Ironically, the very path of sorrow Joseph had traveled became his path of blessing. Even when it seemed otherwise, God was with Joseph and had been directing his steps.

When we question God's leading in our lives because of unfavorable results, we are leaning on our own understanding. Only God can see the big picture and how He is leading us down paths that He will ultimately make work for our good and His glory. He promises in Romans 8:28, "And we know that all things work together for good to them that love God, to them who are the called according to his purpose."

Trust His Leading

When it comes to the major decisions of life, I honestly don't believe that I can go wrong as long as I am following the Lord. It's not because I'm smart or spiritual; it's because I ask God to direct my steps. He promised He would, and I believe Him.

Principle 3—A Trusting Man Gets Direction

Some years ago, when my wife and I were living in Virginia, I got a call to move to Alabama for a job opportunity. We had a fine house in Virginia, a great church, and everything was good at work. We loved where we were, and we didn't want to move.

At first, I turned down the opportunity without giving it much thought or prayer. But I didn't get just one call—I got several. As we began to pray about it, I sensed the Lord directing this move. I told my wife, and we packed up for Alabama.

Looking back, we can see that this was one of the most significant moves of our lives. In hindsight, we see an incredible chain of events. Had we not moved to Alabama, I never would have met the men who would play a part in establishing a company with me. Had we not started our own company, we would not have sold that company three years later. Had we not sold the company, we would not have had the financial resources to support world evangelism as we do now. Furthermore, had I not sold the company and retired, I would not have had the time to go into full-time Christian work. Had I not retired, I would not have made the missions trip to Nicaragua that changed my life.

You see, out of one simple decision, made solely by trusting God's direction, God worked in ways we never could have foreseen. I'm thankful we trusted God's leading and moved to Alabama.

Confidence Boosters

I hope you are finding your confidence level rising as you see these simple principles—God's conditional promises. We can be sure of God's favor when we follow Him with true hearts. We can be sure of God's blessing when we commit to faithfulness. And we can be sure of God's direction when we trust Him to guide us.

God is good to make these promises. As we follow Him, He takes the responsibility to bless and lead. We don't have to move forward in insecurity and doubt. We simply claim God's promises that He will direct our paths and bless us along the way.

4
Principle Four

A Giving Man Prospers

In Proverbs 3:9–10, God delivers yet another conditional promise: "Honour the Lord with thy substance, and with the firstfruits of all thine increase: So shall thy barns be filled with plenty, and thy presses shall burst out with new wine."

The God who owns the world and everything in it (Psalm 24:1) promises you and me, "If you honor Me, I will honor you." It's as simple as that.

An Insider's Tip

Imagine if I were to tell you that I have a secret stock tip based on inside information and that if you purchased this particular stock, you would double, triple, or quadruple your money. You might question me at first, but if you trusted that I really did have accurate information, you'd buy that stock as quickly as you could. More than likely, you'd buy all you could afford.

Well, I do have an inside tip. It's based on God's promises, but it's confirmed by my experience. Here it is: You can't outgive God.

In Luke 6:38, Jesus promised, "Give, and it shall be given unto you; good measure, pressed down, and shaken together, and running over, shall men give into your bosom. For with the same measure that ye mete withal it shall be measured to you again."

Notice that the promise God will give to us starts with our giving to Him. Our tendency to hang onto our money is easily dispelled when we remember that giving to the Lord is actually an investment.

A Personal Testimony

When I was saved, I didn't know much about giving, and I sure didn't know about tithing. I'm embarrassed to tell you, but at our church in the hills of West Virginia, we actually paid dues to be a member of the church. I didn't have the two dollars a month required, so my dad had to pay it for me. (Of course, this stipulation for church membership is not found in the Bible, but I didn't know that at the time.)

One Sunday, an evangelist came to our church and preached on tithing—giving ten percent of all of your income to the Lord. I was making $1.60 an hour, and my fiancée (who is now my wife) was making $1.65.

After Peggy heard the message, she immediately determined to begin tithing. I wasn't so sure. I didn't think I could afford it, and I figured that since tithing was in the Old Testament, it must not apply to our lives today.

I did want to be right with God concerning my finances, so I studied the matter further. As I studied,

I learned that Abraham tithed long before the law was given (Genesis 14:20), and I saw that Jesus instructed us to give. Based on those discoveries and faith in God's promises to bless my giving, I began tithing.

That was forty-two years ago, and if I have missed paying a tithe on one dollar I've made since, it has been unintentional.

As time went on, I began to give above the tithe. God continued to prosper me each time I gave to Him. By the time I retired, the largest lines on my budget were my giving to the Lord's work. This, of course, is no credit to me; it is simply a testimony of God's faithfulness to bless us when we give.

Someone recently asked me, "Ken, do you make so much money now that you don't tithe?"

Looking back at my hesitancy to tithe when I was making $1.60 an hour, I couldn't help but chuckle. "Are you kidding?" I replied. "I'd be afraid not to tithe. God has blessed my giving, and it's a privilege!"

God Honors Faith

Although I'm thankful for the opportunity to give to the Lord and even though I have seen God bless our giving over and over again, I still sometimes struggle to trust Him.

In 2008 when we were in the process of selling our company, the financial recession hit hard. The stock market crashed, and the housing bubble burst.

We actually had the company sold, but when the recession hit, the buyers backed out. In one week, I watched my 401K savings account get cut by fifty percent and the sale of the company go right out the door.

Several months passed, and it seemed as if the company would never sell. In the midst of this concern, our church conducted its annual missions conference. As I already mentioned, the largest check I write every month is for missions—supporting the spread of the Gospel around the world. But at this point in time, my retirement fund was cut in half, the company wasn't sold, and I had a responsibility to provide for my family and save for the future.

I wasn't looking forward to breaking the news of my decision to my wife.

"Peggy, I hate to tell you this, but I am going to cut our missions donation back. We need the money, and I want to be sure we have something to leave for our kids. I'm going to keep giving half of what we normally give, and I'm going to save the other half."

I felt a little guilty, but it made good sense. I felt sure that Peggy would understand my reasoning and agree.

"I don't think we ought to do that, Ken."

I tried again. "Peg, we've got to save for our future. I'm getting older, and we have to retire eventually."

"Well, you still have a job now, don't you?"

"Yes, I guess I do."

"You do whatever you think you ought to do, but I'm against cutting our missions giving."

I felt a bit irritated with Peggy for not understanding the need to save, but I also remembered how she had encouraged and supported my giving decisions through the years.

When the time came at the close of the mission's conference to write our commitment for the next year, I still hesitated. For a man who has seen God bless giving for so many years, I can't understand why I was so determined to give less. But doubt was playing with my mind, and I failed to focus on God's faithfulness.

Then, sitting there in the pew, I remembered Proverbs 3:9–10 and God's promise that He will make a giving man to prosper. I filled out the card with a higher commitment than we had ever given before and dropped it in the plate.

That was on Sunday night. You won't be surprised to hear that before the end of the week, our company sold. I have no doubt that the speedy sale was God's prospering our faith-filled giving. (And it wasn't even my faith that God blessed—it was my wife's faith!)

You can mark it down on your ledger, a giving man always prospers. No Christian can outgive God. God may not always reward in monetary means, but He always rewards.

For All Your Needs

One of the most giving churches in the New Testament was the church at Philippi. In Philippians 4, Paul commended the giving of these Christians.

> *But I rejoiced in the Lord greatly, that now at the last your care of me hath flourished again; wherein ye were also careful, but ye lacked opportunity. Not that I speak in respect of want: for I have learned, in whatsoever state I am, therewith to be content.... Notwithstanding ye have well done, that ye did communicate with my affliction. Now ye Philippians know also, that in the beginning of the gospel, when I departed from Macedonia, no church communicated with me as concerning giving and receiving, but ye only. For even in Thessalonica ye sent once and again unto my necessity. Not because I desire a gift: but I desire fruit that may abound to your account. But I have all, and abound: I am full, having received of Epaphroditus the things which were sent from you, an odour of a sweet smell, a sacrifice acceptable, wellpleasing to God.*—PHILIPPIANS 4:10–11, 14–18

Notice that Paul refers to the Philippians' giving with two metaphors—fruit and a sweet savor. He told them that the benefits reaped through their sacrificial investment in God's work would be fruit to their account. He also told them that their giving was, like the Old Testament animal sacrifices, a sweet savor to God Himself.

Paul followed this commendation with a promise: "But my God shall supply all your need according to his riches in glory by Christ Jesus" (Philippians 4:19). To the giving Christian, God promises that He will personally supply every need we face. Thus, we can give in confidence, knowing that God will care for our needs.

Participate in the Privilege

Consider the incredible opportunity God provides us through giving. We get to invest in His work, and then He blesses us for it! Truly, giving is a privilege.

I don't see paying taxes or utility bills as a privilege. But giving to the Lord is an eternal investment that I know I will never regret.

Do you want God's hand of blessing on your life? Don't try to hold your resources with a clenched fist. Give, and it shall be given unto you.

Conclusion

So there you have it, four simple principles that God has promised to bless.

A good man obtains favor. None of us are perfect, yet God has promised His special blessing on the Christian who lives wholly for Him. This commitment often requires that we say "no" to the world, yet the favor of God is worth more than the approval of man. In this promise, we have the purest basis for an optimistic view of the future.

A good man obtaineth favour of the L*ord*:
but a man of wicked devices will he condemn.
—Proverbs 12:2

A faithful man abounds with blessing. God elevates faithfulness above talent, intelligence, or education. He promises to not only bless, but to abundantly bless His faithful servants.

A faithful man shall abound with blessings: but he that maketh haste to be rich shall not be innocent.—Proverbs 28:20

A trusting man gets direction. The Christian who is asking God to guide him and who is walking according to the Lord's leadership can move forward with confident surety. Even when circumstances appear to fold under his feet, he can trust that God is directing his steps along a road of blessing.

Trust in the L*ord with all thine heart; and lean not unto thine own understanding. In all thy ways acknowledge him, and he shall direct thy paths.*
—Proverbs 3:5–6

A giving man prospers. The opportunity to give to the Lord's work is an opportunity to invest in eternity. God Himself returns this investment with His blessing. He assures the giving Christian that He will personally undertake the responsibility of caring for his needs.

> *Honour the* LORD *with thy substance, and with the firstfruits of all thine increase: So shall thy barns be filled with plenty, and thy presses shall burst out with new wine.*—PROVERBS 3:9–10

These principles are so simple that even a child can understand them. In fact, they are so simple that even a child can follow them.

Living by these four principles doesn't require extensive understanding of deep theological truths. It only requires simple obedience and faith in God to keep His Word.

Best of all, the promises attached to these principles are not dependent upon our resources. They are absolutely dependent on God—the God who never fails, never lies, and has every resource necessary to fulfill His promises abundantly!

I challenge you to take God at His Word. Determine that you will be:

- A good man—a Christian who purposes to live for God.
- A faithful man—a Christian who leans on Christ and goes all the way for God.
- A trusting man—a Christian who seeks God's direction and does not hesitate to follow it.
- A giving man—a Christian who generously invests in the Lord's work.

Choose to live by these principles. In twenty years—and for eternity—you'll be glad that you did. By then, there will be nothing plainer to you than the reliability of God to keep His promises.

These principles work. God promises to bless them, and He does—every time. Determine to live by them, and you too will experience the blessed life.

Visit us online

strivingtogether.com

wcbc.edu

Also available from Striving Together Publications

Stewarding Life
Paul Chappell
This book will take you on a personal stewardship journey, equipping you to live effectively and biblically. It will challenge and equip you to strategically invest your most valuable resources for God's eternal purposes. Through these pages, discover God's most important principles for managing His most valuable gifts. (280 pages, hardback)

Living Beyond Your Capacity
Paul Chappell
The wonderful Holy Spirit of God desires to come into your life at salvation and unfold a daily work of power, grace, and transformation. He can enable you to live a supernatural life—a life that exceeds your human capacity. You can begin discovering and experiencing the Spirit-filled life today! (208 pages, paperback)

Done.
Cary Schmidt
Specifically created to be placed into the hands of an unsaved person and a perfect gift for first time church visitors, this minibook explains the Gospel in crystal clear terms. The reader will journey step by step through biblical reasoning that concludes at the Cross and a moment of decision. (112 pages, mini-paperback)

strivingtogether.com